dear Qui
Tha
your light! ☺
Hope you enjoy.
♡, nikki

grace and grit

empowering poetry by nikki van ekeren

dear Quiver.
Thanks for sharing your light! :)
Hope you enjoy it! Nikki :)

Copyright. © 2019 Nikki Van Ekeren

All Rights Reserved.

ISBN-13: 978-0-578-43406-3

being exactly
who you are
is the greatest
gift of all.

chapter 1
to sculpt

chapter 2
the current of life

chapter 3
move into your heart space

chapter 4
innocence

mermaid living

chapter one

to sculpt

01

soul groups

you sculpt me
and i will sculpt you.
it may hurt a little
and you may never be the same,
but the art of sculpture takes something away
to create something beautiful and new.

have you sculpted me before?
have we enjoyed creating together?
i imagine so.

you've seen me with eyes that
we do not have access to
in this form.
i have seen you with these same eyes.
this unconditional love,
this bond
transcends the 3d realm.
the pain may seem so great at times
that you may not want to continue this art,
but remember that change is slow,
change is beauty,
and our masterpiece will continue evolving.

we do not create our art for them
or for their eyes,
rather we create for the art of creating.
this process,
this alchemy
is our fuel.
it sparks authentic energy
from a well that never runs dry.

this group that we chose to incarnate into
this rowdy group of souls,
is the gallery in which we show our pieces in.
they create a safe space for us to grow in
and truly see ourselves.
let's emerge within,
and play
and sculpt
our magic.

02

goddess emerge

bursts of lavender
flood my mind's eye.
this color speaks love.
i bathe in it.
amethyst colored
joy
enjoy
let go
receive.
my story tries to control me;
yet, i face it
with loving arms.
i am not "it"
i am pure consciousness.
the longer we live on this planet,
the longer our story becomes.
each day is a page in a chapter
in the book of our life.

i choose to write my story...
and rewrite my past.
i choose to revel in my
present state,

for it has brought me here.
i am vibrating at the highest level that i have
in this incarnation.
i trust this truth.
i know that this frequency will continue to
grow and grow.
i am consciously expanding now
and nothing will stop me.
i am me. i am now.

violet, lavender, purple
new colors emerge from within.
i feel my soul emerging
she is kind
yet ferocious.
she is compassionate
yet fierce.
she is me.
i bow to the soul that i came here with.

03

life is about falling in love with ourselves over and over again

the one you love
and the one you hate
both can serve as mirrors to who you are at
your core.
each rose and each thorn
carve your journey.
one is pleasant and the other is painful,
but each has a purpose.
this journey is about self love.
how to love all aspects of what is inside of
you.

every person's journey
contains its own map
which unfolds in front of
every willing participant.
the first step is sharing in the ownership of the
collective shadow...
admitting your darkness with no shame.
you are a part of this world;
therefore you contain its polarity.
creating a safe space for your uniqueness to
flourish takes time, self will and confidence.

inner growth and self study may appear as
indulgences or odd choices for leisure.
one must hold steadfastly in their pursuit,
addressing the guilt,
the shame,
and the inner battle that will erupt.
daily practices will put out this fire
and allow one to truly hone in on
their unique gifts and tools.
the world will begin to see you
as who you want to be.
you will love yourself
and the world in every shade
that it projects.
self love begins to blossom.

when you cultivate the inner self love
to truly see
you begin to love each and everyone
around you.
the abrasive tone that you
were taught to feel
fades away to reveal a sculptor

making a masterpiece.
those that hurt you
are your teachers.
each moment allows for one to tap
into their higher self
and feel good about their choices.
the accolades will come from within.
the flow occurs.
life is sweet.

you can let your true self surface
and fall in love with yourself
again and again.

04

azul

like the sparkling azul sky,
the psyche opens up and thrives with
opportunity.
the wandering clouds are like
passing thoughts.
the psyche is created in real time
while visiting earth
just like the sky presents itself anew
each morning.
nothing is permanent
all things being temporary.
the soul lassos its accompanying psyche
toward it
with loving force
drawing its human counterpart in.
our psyche strives and
instinctively abides
to human law,
but our soul knows better
and challenges us to rise up.

as we begin to see our psyche as
a malleable tool,

we can be more gentle on
ourselves and others.
the sky cannot guard against smoke
that disrupts its beauty.
how can our psyche rise up when
low energies and trained patterns
ask it to sway from its soul?
intention.
the linear format of the world
methodically notes every wrong and right,
but the soul watches and listens for your song.
can you begin to tune your human instrument
to the same frequency as your soul?
allow your resonance
to shimmer from within.
attract your likeness in forms.
the sky bares witness to your transformation.
its calm and delicate lack of form
allows all things in and out.
your psyche is like this.
don't resist.
dive into life.
sing your note.

05

as i witness

as i reside on this planet longer and longer,
i observe how with more years
come more fears, woes and
unnecessary sacrifices.
the gregarious and brave soul
can become heavy and weighed down by the
ways of the world.
this formerly light hearted being
loses its shine
little by little.
that carefree youth
becomes old and scared.

as i witness this pattern,
i also see the opposite.
those who allowed fear to stop them
in the past with their uneducated eyes,
have used their time on this earth field
to grow wiser.
they've learned how
to transmute the low
energy of the world
into high vibratory love.

when in the midst of adverse
worldly circumstances,
they go inside
and take their time to respond.

time is a gift
not a foe.
allow it to change you
into the greatest version of you imaginable.

06

why

why do we hurt the ones we love
when we question the masses?
why do we forget years of experience
when one chooses a different road than us?
why do we listen to one
and judge another?
why do we long for a sense of identity
when our very essence radiates more
uniqueness than any label could.
why do we assume the worst
when goodness and the pure unbridled joy of
truth takes time to emerge?
why are we quick to point a finger
when we should look within?
why do we continue to share low energy with
one another
while love is the easiest form of vibration to
cultivate?
why?
i suppose that this is the human condition
and asking questions allows one to see
the repetitive nature of its journey.

07

trading in the old

this passion
this desire
this trading in of the old
for newness
is everything.
such a climb is so exhilarating.
yet, it can be so lonely.

our eyes take time to see.
this is why we must not stop climbing.
the pain. the uncertainty.
we persist.
we climb.
we continue.
i see now.
i shall never be frightened to trade in
the old
for new.

08

i choose the woman i am

i have witnessed many women before me
and am grateful for their journeys.
i get to choose which aspects
of their lives and personalities
i would like to personify within me.
i get to see things in ways
that their eyes could not.
i get to allow new truths to surface within
and watch alchemy change me.
i am no better or worse,
i just have more resources in which
to sculpt
my being with.

09

grace

you can't control your thoughts,
but you can control your actions.
ask for grace
before you act.
it is truly that simple.

anything that ignites a trigger response within,
represents an issue that your soul
is working on
in this lifetime.
honor your soul's plight.
honor your body's reaction.
react to challenging circumstances
in a way that
will make your future self proud.

10

i am free

after years of walking into a cage,
i am free.
i forgot how
to see me
in the context of this world.
i thought that i had to work
to strain
to extract
to exhibit
my value at every moment.

this life is interwoven
within the miraculous tapestry
of all life.
as long as i am human,
i will have bouts of forgetting
who i am,
my power
my brilliance
but now i know
how to not
identify
with this feeling.

i shall not waiver
regardless of my ability to remember
who i truly am.
i shall float,
wander,
fly,
through life.

11

peeling back the layers

to acknowledge the multitude of layers
we've acquired through conditioning,
opens a gateway.
these layers
have been our invisible anchor to the past.
our story seems to show up in front of us
while we try to write our newest chapter.

we long to change,
but we continue to connect on a
lower vibratory chord.
we want to enhance our abilities to connect
with the invisible realms,
but our habitual patterns make our attempts
haphazard and futile.

this cycle will continue
until we shine a light on it.
the light brings forward the shadow and
lets it heal.
the truth will set your being in flight.

jump into the water feet first

and fully submerge your entire body,
your entire soul.
let the splash
jolt your senses awake.
feel the crisp cool sting of the elements
around you.
merge with it.

begin to reach.
begin to connect from that higher vibration.
begin to project your presence with depth
and confidence.
gather nourishment from your own soul.
this newness will shine a light within and
around
and you will see
your past differently.

all challenges acted as the sculptor
and you are the emerging sculpture.
your beauty will astound you
with its simplicity and grace.
your you-ness is now your guide.

12

i walk with purpose

as i begin to see the flow,
the energy,
the resonance,
the magic of it all...
i carry myself with a purpose
that projects my presence.
this energetic outflow is not forced,
it organically pours from my being
and attracts people, experiences,
thoughts and objects
that heighten my frequency.

i readily reconnect
with my inner energy
and fill up through this endless source.
i walk with grace and confidence
never struggling with what is presented to me.

i breathe with grace.
i know this action is my constant cord to the
unknown,
the mystery,
the source.

i am the wave
and i am the sea.

i can see,
and feel
the confidence this practice brings.
as i tend to my gifts and my calling,
the world
rolls out the red carpet for me.
a new sense of ease and love
projects from my heart.
i enjoy and feel how
all experiences bring magic and lessons.

13

it's how you see

the energy that propels you forward,
the life inside of you,
the art of how you see the world
is your fuel.
mankind has been improperly trained to think
that
how one is seen
drives you forward.
it is the exact opposite.
focusing on how you're seen
empties the magic out of your soul.

it is about looking and seeing
not about being seen.

once one can truly see,
they see themselves.
this creates a feeling of sheer marvel
at the miracle of our presence.
a lens of objectivity
replaces that of subjectivity.
for one has the foresight to know
that their story is not personal

it is an enhancing process.
it is alchemy that takes place within.

when you can see,
you feel the shift from victim to creator.
you see your own shadow,
but do not need to run from it.
you can run naked through life
feeling no shame.

14

leaving the wound behind

i used to allow my wound to guide me,
to be the filter in which i viewed the world
to be the energy that i clung to.
healing involves allowing
the wound
to alchemize.
why do we think that wounds to the psyche
are always permanent?
why do we carry
our wounds around
as if they are a part of us?

i am leaving the wound behind me now.
i choose to not use
my energy and strength
to bring it into my present.
without this wound,
i am no longer seeing with clouded eyes.
i no longer think that the world
is out to get me
because my wound is not dictating my
external circumstances.

i am leaving the wound behind me now
and allowing my eyes of gratitude to shine
through.
the world does not owe me anything.
i am its humble observer and participant.
as i acknowledge my fellow humans' equal
role,
i grow vertically.
my gratitude increases
and i feel surging amounts of energy
fill my being.
i love my life and honor my role.

15

to sculpt

to sculpt,
one needs malleable clay
and a vision of what the end product
will look like.
to sculpt,
one needs discipline
and a confidence in their ability.

creating a masterpiece
takes passion,
longing
and a devotion to the process.
raw elements
enjoy being transmuted
into something beautiful.
shaping and shifting
and allowing miracles
to emerge
from your hands
is how clay becomes a sculpture.

to sculpt,
one needs to flow

with the magic of it all.
how does it all come together in the end?
one need not explain,
but believe that
a sculpture will be born.

grace and grit

van ekeren

chapter two

the current of life

01

the current of life

bravery is being
happy in the now.
aligning so deeply within
that external influences
do not sway your center.
temptations come and go
whilst your core values remain intact.

bravery is exuding courage and confidence
in the midst of all circumstances.
having control
does not equate to confidence
although this is indoctrinated in us all.

be as soft as water
filling up every space you enter
with the fullness of your presence.
this expansive state of mind
will guide you.
radiate your essence
and let your light shine.

allow this present moment
to be enough
setting no future dates as better.
show up
as messy or clean as you appear to be.
your soul is always pure
and will lead the way when asked.

be happy in the now.
accept the present moment.
allow everything to fall into place.

02

horseshoe

as we become more aware of the fact
that we are vessels
emptying and filling
with our environment around us,
we can lessen the level of judgment on
ourselves and others.
we empty, we fill up.
we empty, we fill up.
our actions, mood and feelings are
a mirror of every thread
that is woven
into the tapestry of our life.

clarity brings wisdom and clear eyes
which can navigate through the echoes
of the past.
negative words that try to grab our beings
by the throat
and freeze our spirit
and dampen our light
are just words.
we are beginning to realize that we are the
force that can ignite these words

or leave them hollow.
hollow words die.
give fire to words of passion
and know that
this focus will guide your life.
your feet will always be protected
from the thorny stones on the earth.

03

i see clearly

i see me.
i see my fears,
my talents,
my joy,
my pain...
my all.
i am as transparent as a tree
standing tall in the woods.
naked, yet strong.
solitary, yet part of everything.
i am this tree
slowly emerging and spreading its wings
absorbing energy and light
and transmuting the air it resides in.
i see clearly the beauty that's all around me.
i do not covet external idealisms
rather i embrace my internal essence.
i see the lower energies
move in and out of each of us
taking charge of those who
do not know how to stay centered
within themselves.
i see the higher energies

inspire others
to new and extraordinary heights.
it is all one journey.
the only pain we experience in life
is generated from within.
it is a conditioned way to view life.
we have all been feeding this pain
to stay a part of the collective.
free yourself from this lie...
all sight is in the eye of the beholder.
rise up
and accept your new vision.

04

the genius within

this genius within
is the ability to create, think
and communicate in ways
directly from the divine source.
this genius is the angelic team
that we are born with.
this team ebbs and flows within
one's human journey,
gathering and dispersing angels...
but the core of angels will remain the same.
angels are beyond time,
so one may have the same angel as their
personal historic hero did.

when we openly align
with the genius within,
one is able to create their dream life
and learns that by doing nothing
everything happens.
it is walking through the gateway
every waking moment
to shed the conditioning,
shed the heavy weight of being human

and send light energy within and around.
to purely connect with your
beautiful inner angelic team
is to completely surrender.
let them speak for you.
let them work through you
and become you.

letting your genius take over
requires complete humility.
look at a child
in complete awe and wonderment
at their reflection, their own self.
they allow themselves
to truly love themselves.
this is what we all long to do.

05

clarity

the power of clarity is intense.
it strikes like a bolt of lightening
when mind, body and soul align.
clarity allows one
to truly see
their intention,
their inner tension,
their heart.
i will be the first to admit
after thousands of words
that i have typed, retyped and read and
re-read...
turning inward
and surrendering to self love
is the climb.

06

what if what we see is only part of the picture

as I begin to see myself
as an archetypal figure
playing out this story that's been unraveling
through many lives,
I see how this life
that I see with my human senses
is only part of the entire picture.
I am a drop of water in my ocean,
in our ocean.
what if I am living here and there
at once?
I am here experiencing
this life in this body
and communicating with
the rest of my soul
and consciousness
through dreams
through thoughts
through awakenings.

we are here on this glorious planet
letting our souls emerge
from the over culture

that was created by a tidal wave of fear.
our intentions are creating our life
in multiple dimensions...
this is where our body feelings
connect to
and within
and throughout.
health is directly connected to our intentions.
without overthinking
or over correcting
choose love.
life is simple.
life is love.

07

air

air.
the angelic kaleidoscopic ether that fills my
body with magic.
i blissfully flow.
blue, yellow, green
sing within!

my intention is self love.
i love all of me,
so that i can love all of you.
i reach for love
and receive love in return.
i hope for me
and i hope for you.
i know and live in abundance and share my
half with you.
life is living through me.
there is no clinging
only flow
and truth
and love.

08

become the air that surrounds you

merge with

and become

the air that surrounds you.

it is you.

you are it.

become the space

that holds all,

the air.

merge into its plane

and begin to observe your human flesh.

how it needs

how it speaks

how it clings to fear

how it clings to joy...

your soul listens to your flesh's desires

and intervenes

on its own time.

your flesh may fight back.

observe it.

let it.

know with your entire being

that your soul

never fights.

your soul flows.
your soul observes this experience
and is learning
and growing
as your flesh reacts in an earthly way.
perhaps you sing,
you scream,
you yell,
you cry...
all responses are of the flesh
and can be an echo of another human.
for we are god's sponges
and we feast upon the images
and words
we immerse ourselves in.

set the intention
to bless the air you breathe as divine
this is your ultimate nourishment.
it will merge within you
and become you.
this will flavor the words

that come from
within and around.

09

the dance of duality

as i look out from this body,
the dance of duality immediately beckons.
it stirs in me
a longing, a hunger
for more.

i long to be me
but i fear what i truly am.
i dance back and forth
between two worlds.
one...
of pure joy and acceptance
and the other of fear and shame.
was this journey built for a specific goal?
can i allow myself to awaken fully...
to have the ability to enjoy this dirty,
yet perfect, dance?

as a human
we are composed of flesh
and SOUL.
yin and yang.
a piece of stardust wrapped in flesh

duality at its finest.
my heart leaps out of my chest
with gratitude
when i accept this dance.
it weeps with sorrow,
when I fight it.
with no answers in sight,
let's dance
with love in our hearts,
letting active participation
be our goal.

10

the small moments

trust in quality
over quantity.
believe that living in the moment
far surpasses
planning ahead.
have faith in others.
if your intention is not fully revealed
its energy will surface.
one life is composed of
several small moments,
let them flow out of you like water.
one dollar earned in integrity
is more valuable than one million
made without.
the wisdom that mother earth shows us
in one instant
can plant more truths in us than
an expensive education.
the small moments of love -
a look, a laugh, a note, a hug, a smile
create the tapestry of LIFE.

11

blue energy

when our eyes change
our lives change.
we begin to see the thread of life
the spark of life
that weaves this whole experience together.
it is simple
it is magnanimous
it is all
it is nothing...
it is love.

12

send love

send out love
to get love back.
this notion of reciprocity
has been taught for centuries.
the golden rule
that creates gold
from our actions.

humanity has the gift
of creating love
from hate.
it happens in an instant
and it happens inside of a wise
and truthful spirit.
one who knows that all experiences occur
within the mind.
when a mind is built on the foundation of love,
the life projected from it
is one of pure beauty.

13

this is the main show

what if our hopes for heaven
and our dreams of the next realm
were distracting us from enjoying this
moment?
what if our work that is intended to secure
our spot in heaven
takes us away from
the perfection of the human journey?

can we let go
of our stories,
our coveted archetypes,
our reasonings,
our failures,
our successes,
to see?

what if this is the main show?

14

she is waiting for you

mother earth,
our life force,
the universe,
our source.
she is waiting for you
to accept her.
she is waiting for you
to allow this life force to flow through you.
you can stand up for your voice,
you can project your art,
you can beautifully express yourself
in the way only YOU can.
you can revel in your gifts
that are unique to your
time/body/soul collaboration.
why are you waiting for other
humans to accept and value you?
most humans understand how to echo,
not how to project a unique voice.
most humans long for conformity,
not uniqueness.
allow this.
do not fight a battle that wasn't designed for

you to win...
the art of being human
is derived from
our source.
she is kind
as are we:
humankind.
take credit for the projection
of your slice of reality.
do it now,
before it's too late!
own your art
own your voice
own your projection.
do not let the voices
of others who claim to be
an authority or expert
cloud your clear vision.

the sky doesn't choose who
to grace with its presence,
just as you shall not discriminate
against humanity.

all are equal souls
existing in unique training suits
called bodies.

van ekeren

chapter three

move into your heart space

01

move into your heart space

set the intention
to let go of the weight of fear.
it may topple you over at first,
but set it free
by your intention.
bring your mind's eye
into your heart.
listen to your breathing,
feel your heartbeat's energy,
feel the warmth in your belly,
feel the spark of life inside your
entire being.
breathe in. breathe out.

release into mother nature's rhythm.
center your thoughts
within your heart space
and allow the linear model of thinking
to become a complete circle...
empty, yet full.
focus on your heart's energy.
it is warm and passionate
and intensely loving.

let objects go
and allow energy in.
rise up within your being.
allow your natural vibration of love
to radiate from your being
allowing you to fully
connect and align
with mother earth and father sky.
believe in who you are
and your deep intimate connection
with all life.

02

show up

life is truly this simple...
show up for it.
as humans, we think that we are steering
this vehicle of LIFE.
when truly
our team of ANGELS and guides
have the clearest route.
they see from above
they know
let them guide...
all you have to do in your human form
is show up
in your heart space
with love as your intention.
show up
to
rise up
with grace and ease.

03

today is anew

rise up and shine.
do you know the good news?
yesterday is dust
and
today
is alive with possibilities.
bring nothing into today
that you do not want.
love your life,
your body,
your community,
your talents and gifts...
love it all.
love the thrill of not knowing.
rest into life
for today
is a miracle.
cease planning and worrying.
fall into the arms of the the all
with your heart wide open.

04

ask

ask to thrive
instead of survive.
ask to battle the
internal craving
to hold onto
yesterday's pain and struggle.
ask to rise up
in all circumstances.
ask to transmute every cell in your body
to vibrate on the highest levels
of love and light.
ask to truly love yourself in this moment
and not crave more.
ask to know at all times
who you are and where you came from.
ask to feel your higher self...
the higher dimension in which you came from.
ask to communicate with your highest self
continually and openly and lovingly.
ask to love and revere your beautiful body.
ask to surrender to life
and not fight your growth.

05

crawl out from the web

do we create a web of beliefs
that we trap ourselves in?
do we feel controlled by those
we think are watching us?
tangled in this web,
i stop trying to escape.
i surrender my will.
i accept my vulnerability.
i open my heart.
why have i always felt that everyone
is plotting against me?
is this attack coming from my insides?
why do i want to destroy myself
over and over again?
my soul knows better
but my flesh is weak.
this duality is life as a human.
i rest in this discomfort.
i stop trying to resist it.

i fall to the ground
to the bottom of the pit.
i realize that this fall

allows me to escape from the web of fear
and embrace my heart,
my vulnerable side.
i join my fellow humans on the ground.
it is not so bad here.
i allow my flesh to show me its needs
and i choose
which to act on.
i am not a victim of myself or anyone else.
i allow myself to
rise up
and surrender to this journey.

my senses are squeezing out
from beneath my flesh
embracing the limits that
this dimension has created for us.
there is harmony within this.
i allow the music to come out of me...
out of every pore in my being.
i am singing now.

06

painting the story of life

if love had a color
and fear had a color
and i had a paintbrush to paint
the story of my life,
what color would my painting be?
love is a creation.
fear is an echo.
we can create love
by projecting the energy from our heart,
we create a completely unique
work of art.
we are painting
the story of our life.
i used to think that love
came from the outside.
now,
i know
that i am love.
i am an overflowing fountain of love,
self love
and love for all.

the energy we project into the world

is palpable,
it is felt within and around.
we are constantly creating energy from
within
which flavors our entire life,
being,
and outside world.
we must go within and
begin creating with love.
this is how we paint the masterpiece
of our life.

07

looking back

with time and a clearer lens,
we can all see
how
our lives have
been a series of
absolute miracles.
miracle after miracle
have emerged in the midst
of all experiences.
synchronicities ooze
out of every story.
it is humbling to view
the perfection
of it all.

08

the breeze

soft, cool air whirls around me.
i hear the invisible strength
of the wind
rustle through the trees.
the perfect symphony of sound
permeates through this
magical air.
there is peace.
there is calm.
i face inward
and allow my radiance
to be my guide.
numbers speak through the universe,
perfectly weaving our life story
into a melodic flow.

energetic pulses
continually reach out to our
physical and mental bodies.

our actions,
our thoughts,
our feelings

pulse to the beat
of this natural rhythm.
all is change. all is perfect.
the wave of life
beckons.

van ekeren

chapter four

innocence

01

innocence

we are all born innocent.
this innocence is one of the most important
commodities
of our internal world.
it acts as a lens in which
we view of our lives from,
it colors our perspective,
and allows us to unconditionally
love ourselves.

this innocence can dry up
if we do not learn how to
carry it within.
there is no need to guard or shield oneself.

jump into life.
don't shy away from experiences.
show up as the fullest version of you
and fill each and every room
with your presence.
if you sense another is not fond of the note
that you're playing,
march on and forget their preference.

for when you shine your light
and energize your soul,
your innocence continues to replenish itself.

the only one who can take away
your innocence
is you
in how you internally talk to yourself.
the external world barrels into us
moment by moment
leaving those in its path forever changed.
this cycle will continue.
the beauty lies in
how you feel,
how you integrate the years of life,
how you transmute experience
into wisdom,
how you talk to yourself
in the aftermath of a situation.
this gift of our internal world
never leaves our side
and we have the ability to act
and feel

and discern
how we view ourselves.

this noble honor
is not taught,
but it is mimicked
from human to human.
surround yourself with others
who genuinely love themselves,
surround yourself in your own loving energy.
allow your soul to expand and guide you
and watch your innocence project.

02

learn how to get out of your own way

journey within
to learn how to love yourself
and give your soul all it needs.
journey abroad
to experience and merge and radiate.
give both journeys equal energy
for they both will transform you.

one cannot completely retreat into solidarity
nor can one solely thrive on the external
aspects of life.

when you learn what you
came here with...
your quirks, your tendencies, your gifts.
you can integrate these traits into
the flow of your life.
if you are fighting internally,
life will feel blocked.
when you open up to who you truly are
you will stop the fight and become pure love,
self love.

by journeying within
you can journey beyond.
you will watch as life encourages you
and supports you.
there will be no need to compare
because your sense of inner worth
will carry you.
you will be able to look back and see that
the only one
holding you back
was you.

03

you hold the key

the thoughts you process
are the key
to who you are.
you can allow others' projections
and worries
and fears
steer you
or you can let their words go.
the world meets you where you are,
not where you were
or where you want to be.
the current thoughts
in your mind
are yours.
choose what words you listen to
and how you integrate them into your life.
if one tries to use their words to try
to manipulate,
you hold the key in choosing
how external ideas
seep into your psyche.
use the art of discernment
to guide you.

04

becoming a pioneer

those of us who have never fit in,
or have longed for acceptance,
can finally take a rest.
the natural separation that occurs
when i feel different from you
aches at my heart and my insides.
i have been working so hard for so long
trying to figure out how to fit in.
i have been trying to learn your language
and master it
and show you
with hopes that you will accept me.
this way of living has been exhausting.

i allow myself to wake up,
to see that i have a different frequency
than most,
and to vibrate at my highest potential
with no fear.
my trained mind has tried to
steer my course
insinuating that if i act differently
than the tribe

that i will be ostracized.
i let this go.
i allow myself to be
the pioneer that i know i am.

05

rest

allow
rest
to be a habit.
for it is a strong energy
and may
produce
greater results
than work alone.
rest
to create.
rest
to produce.
rest
to grow.

06

being a light worker

we are the consciousness workers
elevating the energy
lifting the vibration.
when you tap into your true essence,
the journey opens up.
pain doesn't hurt so badly,
JOY magnetizes and attracts,
the FLOW guides.

having a light within is a birthright.
sharing this light with others is an honor.
do not bow down to those who do not want to
experience your light.
do not stop radiating at your fullest when you
feel alone,
rather, journey inside to the deepest regions,
accept reality,
be content in this moment,
allow others to be exactly who they are,
exude one thought only - gratitude.
this one thought will be the filter
in which you see the world.
this filter will allow you

to continue to do your work.

gratitude cultivates joy,
joy creates health,
health oozes happiness,
happiness is light.

07

writing to right

i write to right
the echoes of the unseen past
that still ring in my ears.
i write to right
the wrong
of choices that were made by
sleeping humans.
i write to wake myself up.

i do not accuse myself or others,
for this is a collective journey.
as i open up to the world,
i learn that others have done so
before me.
they have paved the way
with love in their hearts
with sweat in their brow
and heaviness in their minds.
they chose to rise up
and meet their highest self in the now.

i choose this.
i write to hear myself sing.

i write to listen to my song.
i write to gain clarity within
the symphony of life.
i continue to play
my unique note in a sea of so many...
some light
some dark
knowing that the light is always right.
i write.

08

this life is all for you

if something in your life is not to your liking,
remember that you can
rewrite the script at any time.
do not worry about those
that will be affected by your rewrite,
for they have the means to adjust
their script accordingly.
what do you really want?
how can you believe
in yourself more?
what brings out the playful side of you?
how can you bring together a loving and
supportive community?
how can your gifts help you and the world
around you?
continue to ask yourself questions
and begin to let the answers surface.

if you feel that another human
depends on you
for their courage, their strength and
their eyes to see,
rewrite their role in your life.

it is truly that easy.
if you fear that this will be hard,
it may be.
if you jump into your new role willingly,
you will see how easy it can be.
open up to the possibilities of your heart.
allow your soul to feel safe
so it can expand and guide you.

this life is truly all for you.
believe this truth
and watch yourself soar.

09

watching the world make magic

as i learn to surrender
and receive,
i can see the world more clearly.
i can see the world making magic.
everything is truly a gift.
how do we learn to change our filter?
how can we begin to see change and
challenges as opportunities?
take that first step and try.
then another
and another...
it gets easier.

10

to see the spark

stay alert
to see the synchronicities in life.
share these experiences with
anyone who will listen.
this act shows the universe where you are,
who you are
and that you are watching it make magic.
the universe knows and loves us all,
but we can create our own spotlight
that showcases our uniqueness
when we show up for life with
graceful cunning awareness.

know how to see miracles
and allow the energy of this creative force
to saturate your being.
it is our birthright to share in this spark of life.
after all, we are its co-creators.

when we feel nourished by this energy,
the direction of our lives shifts.
the whole experience becomes an honor,
a thrill,

a beating heart.
we are the beating heart
that pulsates within us.
we are the tree that we sit under.
we are the sky that softly glows above us.
we begin to feel an
authentic awareness
that we've always known was there,
but forgot how to access it.
this awareness brings a
deep and continual growing wisdom
that radiates from within
and allows for
grace in all actions.

we are all that we've ever wanted to be
now.
because we are here.

van ekeren

chapter five

mermaid living

01

mermaid living

i dive through the surface of the water
deep down
to the depths of the ocean.
i leave the surface world behind
and dive deep into my life.

the goals are not external
they are internal.
life is like living underwater...
under the surface
of the conditioning
that comes with the current time,
underneath the illusion.

dive deep with me
like a mermaid.
let's experience the sensation
when one dives underwater...
open stillness, complete silence
and exotic peace.

let us access our
inner dimensional senses.

let us exude our personal beauty
and know our perfection,
our divinity,
our wholeness as humans.
humankind.
this is truly a gift to be here on this earth...
we've allowed the surface to cloud
our ability to know
our truth.
embrace the calmness that comes with the
truth.
the act of sharing your truths may sting,
but this will pass
and you will be left in pure peace.
think of sharing your truth
as creating the courage
to take a huge jump
into an unknown pool of beautiful still water.
it takes an instant
and then you jump.
leap, silence, splash, surrender...
peace.

my truth is your truth
and your truth is my truth.
we are all one.
we are the one who
extends a helping hand
and we are the one
who reaches back and takes it.
let us open our heart,
our hands
and soul
and live as the mermaid does
feeling harmony radiate
from our being.

02

the rain

the powder blue sky
vibrates
perfection.
everyday it presents itself anew,
regardless of yesterday
much as we do when we awaken.
the highs, the lows
are carving,
sculpting
our beautiful souls.
i see so clearly at this moment
who we all are.
we are radiant beings
allowing this dimension
to cleanse us
to wash us
to create us
into golden bodies.

the sounds
the scents
the ecstasy
of this jeweled planet

pull me back.

oh rain...

the wind

and the still glowing pewter sky...

we are all one

beautiful

living

being.

03

sand

grains of life,
grains of sand,
human beings.
think of our existence
on this round globe of life.
we are no more
and no less
than a grain of sand.
we are born as a particle of life,
grow into this flesh body,
die as this flesh body
and then fertilize other
particles of life.

the pattern,
the cycle,
the circle
of life on this beautiful planet
is simple
is perfect.

why do we blossom as matter?
why do we resist the perfection

of our mother earth?

are we here to learn how to
unconditionally love ourselves?
let's try.
look at your life's journey as a perfect cycle.
you were born as a seed
that blossomed and developed perfectly
in its environment.
you couldn't have become anything else
than who you are
now.

as you awaken to your perfection,
your need to control your appearance
your surroundings
your reputation
and the other people you encounter
lessens and softens.
it's almost as if you become
as soft as water.
you go with the flow

letting life live through you
bearing no anger, shame, blame or judgements.
rather,
you bask in awe of this life.

what a gift to have been born into matter
with a conscious.
this miracle of life needs no narration
or gimmick
or anything that may lower its vibration.
this life needs reverence,
respect
and unconditional love
for all life...
for our own life
and for that of all living creatures.

04

what you think you become

the wisdom from above,
from below,
from our guides, teacher and angels
is accessible to us all
in our own unique language.
we must first learn how to take care of
our human package
in which we receive their messages...
lovingly feed, clothe, bathe, attend to
our flesh bodies
so our ears are open to hear
and our eyes are open to see.
perhaps we have been at this awhile
or perhaps we instinctually understand how to
lovingly care for ourselves.
the timing is of no importance,
for when it is intended to learn,
it will be learned and applied.

our team
exists alongside of us...
these infinite nonphysical beings
infuse our being with knowledge and courage

and guidance.
when our physical bodies become
clogged and unworkable,
our body alerts us.
our team is trying to get our attention...
we are approaching life on this plane in an
external way
so our exterior package must be slowed down.
this is the time for reflection
for stillness
for meditation
for solitude.
when one gets sick,
one stays inside and takes time for oneself.
in our current culture,
this is the loudest language our guides can
use.
they may try countless other ways,
but our ears are trained
to listen to the external
to other physical beings for guidance.

our inner dimensional team

is continually working to help us.
contrary to what you may feel through your
flesh,
you know you best.
let this statement rest in your heart
for a moment,
relax your shoulders
calm your breathing...
"i know myself best."
your angels are beside you as read these
words.
talk to them.
ask them questions.
interact with them.
they love you unconditionally and ask nothing
of you
for this is your journey
but alas
they know
that life is lived in our intentions.

they are helping us collectively wake up.

05

the belly of mother earth

the miracles from your belly run wild now,
you beautiful mother goddess
so loving and pure
and sweet
and soft
and supple.
how we need you so...
and how you speak to us
in your own ways.

our incarnation in this flesh body
separates us from you
but you still call to us with love and reverence
and respect.
you are waiting for us...
for our return to love.

our ego pulsates with needs
and wants
and demands
but it is you who speak through the fog
as a lighthouse in the choppy ocean,
telling us to go to the center of the circle

when the ego raises its tone.
so, i plunge
mother earth
into the heart of you
into the center of it all...
i give up my story
for our story.
i trust you.

06

reach

your current circumstances
may not be ideal,
but let the action play out
on this earth plane
as it may.
reach,
reach down
deeper
to your emotions.
use your brain muscle to think.
think thoughts of the highest realm
the highest vibrations.
this can be done at all times.
in pure ecstasy
in sheer horror
this package will break open at one point and
your soul will fly away.
for now
let's fly
inside of our flesh bodies...
soaring high.

07

poetry writes itself

the words that i write
created their message long before my hand
touched the page.
the words that i write
are my observations from the lens as i embody
this human...
this hungry soul
who feasts on cosmic food.
being a spiritual warrior,
i have had to learn how to navigate this world.
my inner guidance has prompted
my words to save me
from circumstances that
would not incubate growth.
on earthly scales,
i may tip back and forth,
but on my spiritual journey
i am climbing every mountain.
my soul, body, mind and heart are aligning,
allowing my personality to feed my soul.
green growth
yellow change
blue wisdom...

alchemy within and around.
the past changes as i change.
my perception elevates
and my digestion of the outside
elevates as well.
love is all around me,
i am love.
this poetry will continue to write itself
as miracles are our everyday...
angels, i hear your knowledge
and infuse it with the highest intent,
LOVE.
this creates wisdom
which then fosters transmutation
of the low
to the high.
this poetry
is a blueprint in
how to rise up.

08

the journey home

we are all on a journey home,
to ourselves.
we know that we have never left our
heartspace, our soul, our home,
but this journey strengthens the parts of our
soul that need healing.

we journey together as one.
one universe,
one soul,
one song,
one heart.
yet, our eyes see division
where in fact there is only divinity.

we all go through a time of searching.
as earthly humans
this is manifested as bad behavior
or anxiety
or fear
or pain.
let this flow through...
something inside of you needs it.

i know it hurts,
but let it happen.
focus on where you would like to be
and then let that vision manifest.
all souls are journeying
and will have their unique phases of healing
on our earthly plane.
healing looks painful and is depicted as a
struggle;
it is actually beauty.
the beautiful soul shines
in the darkness and in the light.

09

rocket

i am not the women you thought you knew
i am a rocket.
so full of life
bursting with vitality
rambunctious in nature
eager to confront
ready to bare my soul...
openly
willingly
with no need to hold anything back.

i am emerging as my true authentic self.
i open up my entire book
every page of every chapter...
here i am.
i will share with you my secrets
my strategies
my ideas
my creations
with love
and trust.

this is it! this is my dream,

our dream.
there is abundance.
miracles are our normal way of existence.
.   i unzip miracles
out of thin air.
this is life now.

the cosmos are
a reflection of our inner world
we can look up and see our insides...
how they work,
their tendencies,
their magnetic attractions,
their will,
their grace.

10

the magic in the air

i have often spoke of the air
this magic ether that surrounds our
entire life system.
this air,
it is our most precious resource.
without it
nothing would exist on our
beautiful mother planet.
this air,
holds our consciousness within its belly.
it is our most vital nourishment.

oh air...do we thank you enough?
can i swim through you for the rest of my life
with gratitude?
can i let you give me abundance
through miracles?

how is it that when we plant a seed in the
darkness...with very little air...
the sun's rays find it
and the seed blossoms into life.
this miracle is our nature.

we were born in darkness
and then we wake up.
this metaphor is our truth.
we choose to see it in our own
unique language.

the darkness is the
fertilizer for our light body to emerge from,
to ascend old ways,
to rise up,
to transmute,
to soar.

the magic is in the air.
believe this truth now
and let your logical mind catch up later.
who needs logic anyway?
"not i," said the sun.
"not i," said the moon.
they govern our lives...let us follow the sun
and the moon's lead.
let us allow the magic back into our lives!

11

letting life in

the echoes surface continuously
from generations past
inviting me to challenge their origin
and their role in my life.
how many times have we been through this?
as i engage more with the fears
and face them
and coexist with them,
i feel my frequency rising.
i am me
now
and then
and forever.
i communicate with my past, present and
future self.
i gather strength from the source
that sparks inside of me.
echoes
are the agents of alchemy,
the wood in my fire,
the constant fuel
inspiring me to dig deep within
and challenge the voice.

i know who i am...
who we are.
we are limitless.

echoes,
i challenge you.
echoes,
i identify your lineage.
i allow life in,
in all its glory.

12

still wandering

if i was looking for an ending
or a goal within eyesight,
i have learned the this search is
a conditioned attitude.
the end is death.
the goal is life.
how can one way of living be
better than the next?
how can more of one thing increase
your ability to love?
why did i question my love of wandering?

oh, i know why...
because i was told so.
those seemingly helpful folks
who tell you what to fear,
what to dread
and how to prepare for the worst
meant no harm.
but, they have not realized
how their words flavored lives
with the most bitter taste.

wandering within this journey of life
doesn't mean doing so with blind naivety;
rather, it beckons the call from the soul
to overcome fear based echoes.
fearful words have
been thrown
at us since our inception.
as we awaken, we have the ability
to label them as such,
witness their source
and change the way in which we digest fear.
awareness. alchemy. growth. peace.
i vow to keep on wandering
seeking truth, light and love,
never running from fear, but facing it.
those folks who throw
fearful slogans my way...
i have the ears to detect your lower vibration
now.
this discernment is a tool
that takes a permanent place
on my tool belt for life.

stories continue to repeat
until we understand
that we are the authors.
i lovingly take the pen
to continue writing the story of
my life...
with a zesty gratitude
and a heart for wandering.

13

to celebrate life

we work so hard to "fix" our outside world
so our inside world will feel better,
when life is actually the opposite.
when you begin to celebrate life
and celebrate yourself
exactly as you are,
your lens changes.
you start to see your idiosyncrasies
as beautiful features of an
ever growing human experiment.
you begin to acknowledge habits
that are no longer serving you.
you shine the light on old conditioning
that subconsciously holds you back.
you start to realize that life isn't about
becoming a better version of yourself;
it's a celebration!
a celebration of the
perfect circumstances
that brought you here.

Made in the USA
Middletown, DE
17 January 2020

83306982R10073